Classics on Stage

A Collection of Children's Plays based on Children's Classic Stories

Julie Meighan

First published in 2016 by

JemBooks

Cork,

Ireland

http://drama-in-ecce.com

ISBN: 978-0-9568966-8-1

About the Author

Julie Meighan is a lecturer in Drama in Education at the Cork Institute of Technology. She has taught Drama to all age groups and levels. She is the author of the Amazon bestselling *Drama Start: Drama Activities, Plays and Monologues for Young Children (Ages 3 -8)* ISBN 978-0956896605, *Drama Start Two: Drama Activities and Plays for Children (Ages 9 -12*) ISBN 978-0-9568966-1-2 and *Stage Start: 20 Plays for Children (Ages 3-12)* ISBN 978-0956896629.

Table of Contents

Introduction

Classics on Stage is a collection of ten plays adapted from popular and cherished works of children's literature. This is a unique collection of scripts that will entertain and educate readers. The plays are written with a sense of fun, which will engage and delight children of all ages. There are many ways to approach the plays in this book.

Performance: The plays can be performed in front of an audience. All of the scripts contained in this book maybe freely copied, shared or performed for educational and/or non-commercial purposes. Each play is between 10 and 30 minutes long. Each play can be adapted to suit the various needs of classes/groups. The characters are clearly set out at the start of each play; however, the cast list is flexible, and more characters can be added and existing characters can be changed. All suggestions for stage directions are included in brackets and italics.

Readers Theatre: The scripts can be read in class. The parts can be divided among the readers. No memorisation, costumes or movement is necessary. The plays can be used to promote reading, practice fluency and build vocabulary.

Reading Independently: The plays can be read independently outside of the class. Using the scripts for this purpose will serve to introduce children to the classics and require them to solve any literacy issues they may have without adult assistance, such as deciphering word meanings using context clues.

Plays

The first play in this collection, *The Wizard of Oz,* was adapted from L. Frank Baum's book *The Wonderful Wizard of Oz.*

About the Author:

L. Frank Baum (1856-1919)

Lyman Frank Baum was born on May 15, 1856, in Chittenango, New York. After stints as a newspaper journalist and a grocery store owner, he wrote his first book *Father Goose, His Book* in 1899. In 1900, he wrote the popular and best-selling book *The Wonderful Wizard of Oz*. He went on to write thirteen more Oz books before his death in 1919. His stories have formed the basis for classic films such as *The Wizard of Oz* (1939) starring Judy Garland and *Oz the Great and Powerful* (2013).

The Wizard of Oz

Characters: Dorothy, Uncle Henry, Auntie Em, Toto, Good Witch of the North, Munchkins, Scarecrow, Tinman, Lion, Wicked Witch of the West, Chief of the Flying Monkeys, Flying Monkeys, Emerald City Guard, the Wizard of Oz.

Scene One: Kansas
(Curtains open, Uncle Henry is in the farm yard chopping wood).
Dorothy: *(walks on stage)* Hello, Uncle Henry. What are you doing?
Uncle Henry: I'm chopping wood for the fire so we can be nice and warm this evening. Where have you being?
Dorothy: We went to the woods for a walk and picked some flowers for Auntie Em and had a paddle in the stream.
Uncle Henry: Who were you with?
Dorothy: Why Toto of course! Toto, Toto come here boy.
(A little black dog runs in.)
Uncle Henry: I wish all the animals on the farm loved me as much as that dog loves you.
Dorothy: I love him too.
Uncle Henry: I know you do. (*He continues chopping the wood and Dorothy and Toto play with each other.)*
(Auntie Em walks on stage.)
Auntie Em: Oh Henry, I hope you have put all the animals away for the night. It looks like a big storm is coming.
(*They all look anxiously towards the sky and the light darkens.)*
Uncle Henry: Dorothy, come and help me put the animals away and Em, you get us some food and water. We will need it because the storm looks like it might turn in to

a cyclone, so it's a good idea that we spend the night in the cellar.
(They all leave the stage. Lights get dark, sound of wind and thunder.)
(Dorothy, Henry and Toto all come back on the stage.)
Henry: Everything is locked up for the night. The cyclone is coming, so we better join Auntie Em in the cellar.*(Henry runs off the stage, but then there is a sudden crash of thunder and Toto gets scared and runs the opposite way. Dorothy runs after him. The cyclone has come and the lights flicker on and off. Dorothy finally finds Toto and they are thrown around the room until eventually Dorothy hits her head and is thrown to the floor. The sound continues on for a while and then there is a crash and everything is in darkness.)*
(Curtains close)

Scene 2: Munchkin Land
(The Munchkins come in from the back of the theatre. They will improvise and interact with the audience. They will tell the audience about the Wicked Witch of the East who treats them like slaves and her sister the Wicked Witch of the West.) (Dorothy wakes up and a bird is singing and the sky is clear and blue.)
Dorothy: Uncle Henry, Auntie Em where are you?
(She gets up slowly and walks out and sees some Munchkins and the Good Witch. They all bow when they see Dorothy, but the Munchkins run away and hide.)
Good Witch: You are most welcome to Munchkin Land.
(All the Munchkins start giggling but Dorothy can't see them.)
Dorothy: Why thank you, everybody; you are most kind.
Good Witch: No, thank you so much for killing the Wicked Witch of the East. Now all the Munchkins are free from her power.
Dorothy: I think there must be some mistake. I didn't kill anyone.

Good Witch: *(She points to the house)* Well, your house did.
Dorothy: Oh dear, I didn't mean to kill her.
Good Witch: You don't understand; it is a good thing because now the Munchkins are free from her power.
Dorothy: Who are the Munchkins?
Good Witch: They are the people that live in the land of the East. They were the Wicked Witch of the East's slaves. And now they are free. Munchkins, come out, come out where ever you are and meet your saviour.
(Munchkins come out from where they are hiding and they go and examine the dead witch.)
Munchkin 1: She is well and truly dead.
Munchkin 2: There is nothing left of her, except her ruby slippers.
Munchkin 3: Well done, Dorothy, you are new queen of Munchkin Land.
(They all sing, "Ding dong the witch is dead," and do a dance.)
Dorothy: But I want to go home to my farm in Kansas. I don't want to be the queen of this place. *(She starts to cry.)*
Good Witch: Well Dorothy, you are not in Kansas anymore. *(She comforts her.)*
Dorothy: But how do I get home to Uncle Henry and Auntie Em and the farm?
Good Witch: You must go to the Emerald City and ask the great and powerful Oz to help you.
Dorothy: Who?
Good Witch: He is a wonderful wizard who knows everything. He will help you.
Dorothy: But how do I get to Oz?
Good Witch: You must walk. It is a very long journey through a land that is sometimes pleasant and friendly but sometimes very dark and terribly scary. But here, take the Wicked Witch's ruby slippers. They will keep you safe. All you need to do is follow this yellow brick road.
(They all sing, "We are off to see the wizard." They all leave the stage, and there is darkness. Dorothy walks on

stage and there is a scarecrow on the stage. She walks past him but the scarecrow winks at her and she returns and looks at him and then thinks she has just imagined it so she walks on.)

Scene 3: The Yellow Brick Road
Scarecrow: Hello there!
Dorothy: *(Stops walking.)* Did you speak?
Scarecrow: Yes I did. Can you help get me down from this perch? My arms are very stiff.
(Dorothy helps him get down.)
Scarecrow: That's much better. Thank you. What's your name?
Dorothy: Dorothy
Scarecrow: That's a nice name, Where are you going, Dorothy?
Dorothy: I'm going to the Emerald City to ask the wizard how to get home to the farm and to Uncle Henry and Auntie Em.
Scarecrow: Where is the Emerald City?
Dorothy: I don't know *(pauses);* I thought you would know.
Scarecrow: I don't know anything because I don't have a brain. *(Pauses.)* I know, if I come to the Emerald City with you, do you think the wizard will give me a brain?
Dorothy: I don't see why not. Come with me. But we must find the yellow brick road.
Scarecrow: What's a yellow brick road?
Dorothy: A road made with yellow bricks.
Scarecrow: Look, there it is. *(He points to the yellow brick road.)*Oh Dorothy, you are so clever.
(They sing, "We are off to see the wizard." They go off stage. When they come on stage again, there is a tin man.)
Dorothy: I'm so tired, Scarecrow. I must rest.
Scarecrow: We can rest here.
(They both sit down and Dorothy starts to sleep. There is a loud groan and it startles Scarecrow.)

Scarecrow: What's that? Dorothy, wake up!
(Dorothy wakes up. There is a loud groan again.)
Dorothy: What's that?
(Tin Man makes a creaking sound. He is made completely of tin and he holds an axe over his shoulder. They both come around him and look at him.)
Scarecrow: Did you say something?
Tin Man: I've been groaning to catch your attention. I've been groaning for more than a year but no one has heard me.
Dorothy: Why, whatever is the matter? How can we help you?
Tin Man: Get that oil can over there and oil my joints. It rained about a year ago and I got rusty and ceased up.
(Dorothy oils him and he moves his body slowly.)
Tin Man: That's so much better. I feel like a new man. Thank you so much. I'd have rusted completely if you hadn't helped me. I'm so glad you came by. Where are you going?
Dorothy: We are off to see the Wizard of Oz in the Emerald City. I want him to help me get home.
Scarecrow: And I want him to give me a new brain.
Tin Man: I want a heart because I'm nothing but empty tin inside. Do you think he would give me a heart?
Dorothy: Why don't you come with us?
Scarecrow: There is no harm in asking.
(They sing, "We're off to see the wizard," and they leave the stage. They come back on the stage. It is getting dark. They hear a lion roar.)
Dorothy: What's that?
Scarecrow: I'm scared.
Tin Man: It sounds like a wild beast.
(Lion runs and roars at Scarecrow; he hits him with his paws and knocks him over. Then he jumps on Tin Man and roars again and knocks him over. He roars at Dorothy who has Toto next to her. They are both frightened. Dorothy suddenly hits the Lion on the nose and he backs away and starts to cry.)

Dorothy: You should be ashamed of yourself.
Lion: *(Still crying.)*But I didn't hurt anyone.
(He starts to help Scarecrow and Tin Man up.)
Lion: I'm sorry. Did I frighten you? I was much more frightened myself.
Tin Man: A cowardly lion.
Scarecrow: I never heard of such a thing.
Lion: I was born a coward. It wouldn't matter very much, but a lion is the king of the beasts and all the other animals in the forest expect me to brave. All the other animals laugh at me for not being brave. *(He wipes away his tears with his tail.)*
Dorothy: Perhaps we can help. We are going to the Emerald City to see if the Wizard of Oz can help me get home.
Scarecrow: And give me some brains.
Tin Man: And give me a heart. Come with us and he may be able to give you some courage.
Lion: What a great idea. I will come with you.
(They all go off stage singing, "We are off to see the wizard.")
(Enters Wicked Witch with an evil chuckle)
Wicked Witch: So you think you are going to see the Wizard of Oz do you? Not if I have anything to do with it. Monkey, come here!
(The chief of the flying monkeys comes in very slowly carrying two books.)
Wicked Witch: What's wrong with you? *(She hits him.)*
Chief Monkey: I was sleeping.
(Witch hits him again.)
Wicked Witch: That will wake you up. Now, where is my book of spells? (*Monkey gives it to her.)*
Take three onions and some garlic. *(She stops and looks angrily at the monkey.)* What is this?
Chief Monkey: Your book of smells. It is what you asked for.
Wicked Witch: *(Hits him again.)* I said *spells* not *smells*. Book of spells. (*He gives her the other book.)*

Wicked Witch: Make a field of poppies that are beautiful but deadly to make sure our friends never reach the Land of Oz.

Scene 4: The Poppy Field
(They walk into the poppy field.)
Dorothy: What beautiful flowers. *(She smell them.)*
Scarecrow: I suppose so. When I have brains I will probably like them better.
Tin Man: If only I had a heart I would love them better.
Lion: I always liked flowers. They seem so helpless and frail. But there are none in the forest as bright as these. *(He starts to yawn.)* They make you sleepy.
Dorothy: I'm suddenly very tired.
Lion: Oh dear, the smell of the flowers are killing us. I can't keep my eyes open.
Scarecrow: We are not made of flesh so it can't kill us, but we have to get Dorothy, Lion and Toto out of here quickly.
Tin Man: Lion, run as fast you can out of here; take Toto with you, and we will get Dorothy.
Scarecrow: Let's make a chair with our hands and carry her. *(They carry her off stage.)*
(Wicked Witch comes back on stage and she is looking at her crystal ball.)
Wicked Witch: Monkey, come here. NOW!
Monkey: Yes.
Wicked Witch: Can you see anything?
Monkey: Four travellers and a dog.
Wicked Witch: Four more?
Monkey: No, they are the same ones.
Wicked Witch: That's impossible. Nobody could get through the poppy field.
Monkey: Perhaps they are cleverer than you.
Wicked Witch: Impossible.
Monkey: Then, perhaps they are stronger than you.
Wicked Witch: Nobody is stronger than me.

Monkey: Then, why are they still on their way to see the wizard?
Wicked Witch: I don't know. But I will stop them. Call the army of flying monkeys.
(Flying monkeys enter and they dance menacingly around the stage. After they leave, Dorothy and her friends enter from the back of the auditorium. The curtains are closed.)

Scene 5: Outside the Emerald City
Dorothy: Have you noticed something?
Lion: Everything is getting greener.
Tin Man: I think we must be near the Emerald City.
Scarecrow: Here is the door. Someone is coming. Can you hear footsteps?
Guard: What do you want?
Dorothy: We have come to see the great Oz.
Guard: No.
Dorothy: Why not?
Guard: Oz is powerful and terrible. If you come on a foolish errand and bother him whilst he is busy, he might be angry and destroy you all in an instant.
Scarecrow: But it isn't a foolish errand or an idle one.
Tin Man: But it is terribly important.
Dorothy: And we were told he was a good wizard and that he would help us.
Guard: So he is and he rules the Emerald City wisely and well. But to those who are not honest or who approach with curiosity, he is most terrible.
Dorothy: But we must see him.
Guard: Okay, then. If you are sure. But everything is green inside. Put on these sunglasses.

Scene 6 – Inside the Emerald City
(The curtains open and there is smoke and everything is green. They can't see the wizard but they can hear his voice.)

Wizard of Oz: I'm Oz, the great and powerful. Who are you? And why do you seek me?
Dorothy: I'm Dorothy, the small and meek. I have come to you for help.
Oz: Where did you get those ruby slippers?
Dorothy: I got them from the Wicked Witch of the East when my house fell on her and killed her. The Good Witch of the North told me you would help me.
Oz: What do you wish me to do?
Dorothy: Send me back to the farm in Kansas where my Uncle Henry and Aunt Em are. They will be very worried about me. I've been away for such a long time. .
Oz: Why should I do this for you?
Dorothy: Because you are strong and I'm weak.
Oz: But you are strong enough to kill the Wicked Witch of the East.
Dorothy: That was an accident. I didn't mean to.
Oz: Well, you have no right to ask me to send you back to Kansas unless you do something for me. Help me and I will help you.
Dorothy: What must I do?
Oz: You killed the Wicked Witch of the East; now kill her sister and I will think about helping you and your friends.
Dorothy: But I never killed anything willingly. How do I kill the Wicked Witch of the West?
Oz: Until the Wicked Witch dies, you will never see your aunt or uncle again. If your friends help you, I will grant their wishes of some brains, a heart and some courage. But you must bring proof she is dead.
(Curtains closes and Dorothy, Toto, Scarecrow, Tin Man and Lion are in front of the stage.)
Dorothy: What will we do?
Lion: There is only one thing we can do and that is go to the west of Oz and find the Wicked Witch and destroy her.
Dorothy: Suppose we can't?
Lion: Then I will never have courage.
Scarecrow: And I will never have brains.
Tin Man: And I will never have a heart,

Dorothy: I suppose we must try.
Lion: I will go with you but I'm too much of a coward to kill the witch.
Scarecrow: I will come too, but I won't be much help because I'm such a fool.
Tin Man: I haven't even have a heart to harm the witch.
(They go off to the back of the auditorium and go out the door.)

Scene 7: The Witch's Castle
(Curtains open and the witch is it at her cauldron making a spell.)
Witch: Spin, spin, spin my spell.
Make the winds their secret tell.
Spin, spin, spin.
Monkey, monkey, come here.
Monkey: What is your wish, mistress?
Wicked Witch: Get me a telescope.
Monkey: Certainly. Where is it?
Wicked Witch: If I knew where it was, I wouldn't ask you?
(He searches everywhere and eventually he finds it. He returns with it, Witch grabs it off him and looks in it.)
Wicked Witch: I see the four travellers and that pesky dog again, and they are coming this way from Emerald City.
Monkey: What will we do?
Wicked Witch: You will call the army of flying monkeys and tell them to get those four, and the little dog too, and to tear them to pieces.
Monkey: And don't come back until they are all dead.
(The four travellers and the dog come in from the back of the stage.)
Dorothy: We should rest here for the night.
Scarecrow: Yes, let's all go to sleep.
Lion: *(Talking to the audience.)* Everyone, you know I get scared, so if you see anyone that shouldn't be here, shout, "Danger! Danger!"

(They settle down for the night. The monkeys come in from the back and creep up on them.
They wake up and chase them around the stage. Eventually, the monkeys capture all of them. The witch comes on stage.)
Witch: Where did you get those ruby slippers? You are the one that dropped from the sky and killed my beloved sister. I will kill you myself.
(Dorothy breaks free and the witch chases her around the stage. Dorothy eventually finds a bucket and throws the bucket of water over her.)
Witch: Help me, help me! I'm melting. *(She melts to the ground and all there is left of her is her hat.)*
Chief monkey: You killed her.
All the monkeys: Hip, hip hooray! Three cheers for Dorothy.
They all sing, "Ding dong the witch is dead."
(Curtains closes.)

Scene 8: Emerald City
(The four travellers come in from the back stage. They ring the bell.)
Guard: Are you back again? I thought you had gone to visit the Wicked Witch of the West.
Scarecrow: We did visit her, but she melted.
Guard: Melted? What good news! You better come in then.
(They enter Emerald City.)
Oz: I'm the great Oz. Why do you seek me?
Dorothy: We have come to claim our promise.
Oz: What promise?
Dorothy: You promised to send me back to Kansas.
Scarecrow: You promised me brains.
Tin Man: You promised me a heart
Lion: And you promised me courage.
Oz: Is the witch destroyed?
All: YES!
Oz: I'm very busy today. Come back tomorrow.

Tin Man: You had plenty of time already. You must keep your promises.
(Lion roars and Toto gets scared and goes behind the screen and Dorothy runs after him. She pulls a little old man out from behind the screen.)
Dorothy: Who are you?
Oz: I'm Oz, the great and powerful.
(They look at him in disbelief.)
Dorothy: Are you not a great wizard?
Oz: Not a bit, dear. I'm just a common man. I'm from Omaha.
Dorothy: That's near Kansas. How did you get here?
Oz: I came in a hot air balloon. But because I came from the clouds, everyone thought I was great and wonderful. I have no magic powers; that's why I was scared of the wicked witches. They had great powers, which they used for evil. I was willing to promise you anything for you to get rid of her. I'm sorry I can't help you. I'm a good man but a bad Wizard.
Scarecrow: So you can't give me brain?
Oz: You don't need one. You are learning something new every day. Experience is the only thing that brings knowledge. Here, takes this. It's a degree from the University of Life. *(He gives him a scroll and a graduation hat.)*
Lion: What about my courage?
Oz: You have plenty of courage; all you need is confidence to find it. Here, take this medal for bravery. *(He puts the medal around his neck.)*
Tin Man: What about my heart?
Oz: You've shown that you care and that you love Dorothy and her friends, but here, take this and put it where your heart should be. *(He gives him a toy heart and pins it where his heart should be.)*
Dorothy: But how will I get home?
Oz: You always had the ability to get home. All you need to do is click your ruby slippers three times and say there is no place like home.

Dorothy: Goodbye everyone. *(She hugs everyone and grabs Toto.)*
There is no place like home, there is no place like home, there is no place like home.
(Black out.)

Scene 9: The Farm in Kansas
(Dorothy wakes up in her house and Uncle Henry and Auntie Em are next to her.)
Uncle Henry: We were so worried about you.
Auntie Em: You hit your head and were knocked out.
Dorothy: Oh dear, where is Toto?
Auntie Em: He is here.
Uncle Henry: The storm is over and we are all safe.

The next play, *Alice in Wonderland,* is based on the book *Alice's Adventures in Wonderland* by Lewis Carroll.

About the Author:

Lewis Carroll (1832-1898)

Lewis Carroll was the nom de plume of Charles L. Dodgson. Dodgson was born on January 27, 1832, in Daresbury, Cheshire. He had 11 siblings and he was the oldest boy. His father was a clergyman. He excelled at mathematics and was awarded a scholarship to Christ Church where he later served as a lecturer. The book *Alice's Adventures in Wonderland* was published in 1865. It became popular and Carroll wrote a sequel *Alice through the Looking Glass and What Alice Found There* which was published in 1871. By 1932, *Alice's Adventures in Wonderland* was the most popular children's book in the world.

Alice in Wonderland

Characters: Alice, Lorina, White Rabbit, Key, Caterpillar, The Pigeon, Fish Footman, Frog Footman, Duchess, Cook, Cheshire Cat, March Hare, Mad Hatter, Dormouse, Two of Hearts, Seven of Hearts, Five of Hearts. King of Hearts, Queen of Hearts and the Knave of Hearts.

Scene 1: Under the Tree in the Garden

(Curtain closed, Alice and her sister Lorina are sitting on the steps in front of the stage. Lorina is reading a book.)

Alice: Lorina, I am bored. There is nothing to do.

Lorina: It is such a lovely day. Why don't you sit with me under the tree and read your book?

Alice: My book is silly. It is all about a rabbit that talks. I mean, have you heard of a talking rabbit?

Lorina: *(Yawns and stretches.)* I think I will go for a snooze. *(She falls asleep and Alice tries to read her book. Suddenly, from the back of the theatre comes a white rabbit. He is in a panic and looking at his watch.)*

White Rabbit: I'm late, I'm late, I'm late for a very important date.

(He runs past Alice, through the curtains and on to the stage out of sight.)

Alice: *(Looks at audience.)* Did I just see a talking white rabbit? He has just run down a rabbit hole. Do you think I should follow him down the rabbit hole? Mr. White Rabbit, please wait for me. *(She runs after the white rabbit.)*

Scene 2: The Rabbit Hole/The Curious Hallway

(She stands on the stage. It is dark, and she starts to fall into the rabbit hole.)

Alice: Oh my goodness. I'm falling, I'm falling. If I don't stop, I will end up near the centre of earth. I might even end up in Australia where everything is upside down and the wrong way around. Somebody, help me. *(She falls and*

then stops suddenly and she is in a curious hall with a wall in which there is a small locked door.)
Alice: What a curious place this is. I see a really beautiful garden through the key hole, but the door is too small. How will I get in?
Key: Here, use me to open the door.
Alice: I can't because the door is too small for me to fit through.
Key: Drink this. (*Key gives Alice a bottle that has "drink me" written on it.)*
Alice: *(Drinks.)* I'm shrinking. *(Alice is now too small to reach the handle to open the door.)* I will never get through the door now. I'm too small.
Key: Never fear. Eat this piece of cake and you will grow bigger.
Alice: *(She takes a bite out of the cake.)* Curiouser and curiouser! Now I'm opening out like the largest telescope that ever was. Goodbye, feet! Oh, my poor little feet, I wonder who will put on your shoes and stockings for you now, dears? I'm sure I shan't be able! I shall be a great deal too far off to trouble myself about you; you must manage the best way you can. Oh dear, what nonsense I'm talking!
White Rabbit: *(Entering on the run, carrying a fan and some gloves.)* Oh! The Duchess, the Duchess! Oh! Won't she be savage if I've kept her waiting!
Alice: If you please, sir–
White Rabbit: Ahhhh! *(He drops the fan and gloves and runs offstage.)*
Alice: *(Calling to White Rabbit.)* Wait!! *(Picks up the gloves and fan.)*
Alice: Curiouser and curiouser, I'm growing smaller again and now I can get through the garden door.

Scene 3: The Magical Garden
Caterpillar: Who are YOU?
Alice: I—I hardly know, sir, just at present. At least, I know who I was when I got up this morning, but I think I must have been changed several times since then.

Caterpillar: What do you mean? Explain yourself!
Alice: I can't explain MYSELF. I'm afraid, sir because I'm not myself, you see.
Caterpillar: I don't see.
Alice: I'm afraid I can't put it more clearly, for I don't understand it myself.
Caterpillar: Who are you?
Alice: I think you ought to tell me who YOU are, first.
Caterpillar: Why? *(Alice stamps the ground and walks away.)* Come back! I've something important to say! *(Alice returns.)* Keep your temper.
Alice: Is that all?
Caterpillar: No. So you think you're changed, do you?
Alice: I—I'm afraid I am, sir. I can't remember things as I used to. I can't keep the same size.
Caterpillar: What size do you want to be?
Alice: Oh, I'm not particular as to size; only one doesn't like changing so often, you know.
Caterpillar: Are you content now?
Alice: Well, I should like to be a LITTLE larger, sir, if you wouldn't mind. Three inches is such an awful height to be.
Caterpillar: It is a very good height, indeed!
Alice: But I'm not used to it!
Caterpillar: One side will make you grow taller, and the other side will make you grow shorter.
Alice: One side of WHAT? The other side of WHAT?
Caterpillar: Of the mushroom.
(Caterpillar gives Alice the mushroom and exits.)
Alice: And now which is which? (She takes a bite.) Whoa!!!!!
(Pigeon enters.)
Pigeon: *(He pecks ALICE in the head.)* Serpent!
Alice: I'm not a serpent! Leave me alone!
Pigeon: *(He pecks her again.)* Serpent I say again!
Alice: I haven't the least idea what you're talking about.
Pigeon: As if it wasn't trouble enough hatching the eggs, but I must be on the lookout for serpents night and day. I haven't had a wink of sleep.

Alice: I'm sorry you've been annoyed.

Pigeon: And just as I'd taken to the highest tree in the wood and just as I was thinking I should be free of them at last, they must needs come wriggling down from the sky! SERPENT! *(Attacks Alice.)*

Alice: I am not a serpent, I tell you! I'm a...I'm a...

Pigeon: Well! What are you? I can see you're trying to invent something.

Alice: I'm a little girl.

Pigeon: A likely story. I've seen a good many little girls in my time, but never one with such a neck as yours. No, no, you're a serpent, and there's no use denying it. I suppose you'll be telling me next that you've never tasted an egg.

Alice: I have, but little girls eat eggs quite as much as serpents you know.

Pigeon: I don't believe it. You're looking for eggs and what does it matter to me whether you're a little girl or a serpent?

Alice: It matters a good deal to me! But I'm not looking for eggs, and if I was, I shouldn't want yours.

Pigeon: Well, be off with you then. (*Pigeon pushes Alice and she falls.)*

Alice: *(Picks up the mushroom.)* The mushroom, I almost forgot! *(She eats and grows back to her normal size.)*

Scene 4: Outside the Duchess's Palace

Alice: I've got back to my right size. I wonder? *(Sees the door.)* Whoever lives there?

Frog Footman: *(Holding an invitation out to Fish Footman.)* For the Duchess. An invitation from the Queen to play croquet.

Fish Footman: Thank you. *(To Alice.)* There's no sort of use in knocking, and that is for two reasons. First, because I'm on the same side of the door as you are. Secondly, because they're making such a noise inside, no one could possibly hear you.

Alice: How am I to get in?

Frog Footman: There might be some sense in your knocking, if we had the door between us. For instance, if you were INSIDE, you might knock, and I could let you out, you know.
Alice: How am I to get in?
Fish Footman: I shall sit here 'til tomorrow or the next day maybe... I shall sit here, on and off, for days and days.
Alice: But what am I to do?
Frog Footman: Anything you like! *(The door opens and Alice grabs the invitation and runs through.)*

Scene 5: Inside the Duchess's Place
(Cook is throwing plates and cups around.)
Alice: Where is the Duchess?
Cook: She is over there. *(Points to the Duchess.)*
Duchess: Cook, what are you doing?
Cook: I am making soup for lunch.
Duchess: *(To Alice.)* Who are you? And who let you in?
Alice: I'm Alice. The Fish and Frog Footmen let me in. Well they didn't stop me.
Duchess: I have to get rid of them. Cook, remind me to get of rid of the Fish and Frog Footmen.
Cook: I was planning on making fish-frog stew tomorrow, so we need to get new footmen anyway.
Alice: I have an invitation from the Queen.
Duchess: *(Looks at invitation.)*She wants me to go to the croquet game.
Alice: Are you going?
Duchess: I don't know; she usually sends me to the prison tower when I beat her.
Alice: She is a sore loser, then?
Duchess: I must get ready. Cook, come and help me. *(Both leave the stage. Alice sees a Cheshire cat.)*
Alice: Why are you grinning?
Cheshire Cat: Cheshire cats always smile.
Alice: Can you please tell me where I go from here?
Cheshire Cat: Well that depends on where you want to go.

Alice: I don't mind.
Cheshire Cat: Then, it doesn't matter where you go from here.
Alice: Well, what sorts of people live in this direction? *(Points to left.)*
Cheshire Cat: In that direction lives the Hatter and in that direction lives the March Hare. Both of them are mad.
Alice: I don't want to meet mad people.
Cheshire Cat: Oh dear! Don't you know? We are all mad here. You must be mad.
Alice: How do you know?
Cheshire Cat: You must be or else you wouldn't have come here. Are you going to play croquet with the Queen?
Alice: I would like to but I haven't been invited.
Cheshire Cat: Well, I'll see you there.
Alice: I've seen hatters before. The March Hare will be much more interesting, and perhaps as this is May it won't be raving mad—at least not as mad as if it was in March.

Scene 6: The Tea Party

Hare, Hatter, Dormouse: Twinkle, twinkle little bat, How I wonder what you are at. *(Sings twice. Alice tries to join them but they start yelling at her.)*
Hare, Hatter, Dormouse: No room! No room!
Alice: There is plenty of room.
March Hare: Have some wine.
Alice: I don't see any wine.
March Hare: That is because there isn't any. *(All laugh.)*
Alice: Well it wasn't very nice of you to offer.
March Hare: Well it wasn't very nice of you to sit down without being invited.
Alice: It isn't your table; it is set for a great deal more than three.
Hatter: Your hair wants cutting.
Alice: Keep your personal remarks to yourself.
Hatter: The butter has crumbs in it.

March Hare: Well, you shouldn't have put your bread knife in it.
Alice: What a funny watch! It tells the day of the month, and doesn't tell what o'clock it is!
Hatter: Why should it? Does YOUR watch tell you what year it is?
Alice: Of course not, but that's because it stays the same year for such a long time together.
Hatter: Which is just the case with MINE.
Alice: I don't quite understand you.
Hatter: The Dormouse is asleep again.
Alice: Oh what a waste of time. Wake up Dormouse!
Hatter: If you knew Time as well as I do, you wouldn't talk about wasting IT. It's a HIM.
Alice: I don't know what you mean.
Hatter: Of course you don't! I dare say you never even spoke to Time!
Alice: Perhaps not, but I know I have to beat time when I learn music.
Alice: Ah! That accounts for it; he won't stand beating. Now, if you only kept on good terms with him, he'd do almost anything you liked with the clock. For instance, suppose it were nine o'clock in the morning, just time to begin lessons; you'd only have to whisper a hint to Time, and round goes the clock in a twinkling! Half-past one, time for lunch!
March Hare: I only wish it was.
Alice: That would be grand, certainly, but then I wouldn't be hungry for it, you know. Is that the way YOU manage?
Hatter: Not I! We quarrelled last March, just before HE went mad, you know *(indicating Hare)*.It was at the great concert given by the Queen of Hearts, and I had to sing, "Twinkle, twinkle, little bat! How I wonder what you're at!" You know the song, perhaps?
Alice: I've heard something like it.
Hatter: It goes on, you know, in this way: "Up above the world you fly, like a tea-tray in the sky. Twinkle, twinkle—"

Dormouse: (*Sleepily.)* Up above the world you fly, like a tea-tray in the sky. Twinkle, twinkle—"
Hatter: Well, I had hardly finished when the queen jumped up and said, "He is murdering time; off with his head."
Alice: The queen doesn't sound very nice.
Hatter: Since then, he won't do a thing I ask. It is always six o'clock.
Alice: Is that why all the tea things are out?
Hatter: We never get a chance to wash up.
March Hare: I think Alice should tell us a story.
Alice: I don't have a story to tell.
March Hare: Dormouse, tell us a story.
Dormouse: Ok. Once upon a time there were three sisters who lived in the bottom of a well.
Alice: What did they live on?
Dormouse: Treacle.
Alice: They must have been very ill.
Dormouse: Yes, they were very ill.
March Hare: Have some more tea, Alice.
Alice: How can I have more when I hadn't any to begin with?
March Hare: Well, how can you have less, then?
Alice: Why did they live in the bottom of the well?
Dormouse: Because it was a treacle well.
Alice: There is no such thing.
Dormouse: Stop interrupting.
Mad Hatter: I need a new cup; let's all move down a place.
Alice: This is the silliest tea party I was ever at in my life.
(Hatter, Hare, Dormouse shrug their shoulders and run off singing, "Twinkle, twinkle little bat.")

Scene 7: The Croquet Game
(Suddenly a rose tree appears.) (3 playing cards of hearts are painting it.)
Two of Hearts: Be careful, Five, you are splashing paint all over me.

Five: I can't help it; Seven pushed me.
Seven: No I didn't. Why do I always get the blame?
Alice: What is going on here?
Seven: Oh my! You scared us. I nearly lost a year of my life. I nearly became six again.
Two: Well you see, we planted a white rose bush and the Queen wanted a red one. So we are trying to change it before she turns up.
Five: Red alert! Red alert! The Queen is coming.
(Enter King and Queen. They all bow as the Queen inspects the rose bush. She notices Alice.)
Queen: Who is this?
Cards: We have no idea.
Queen: Well, off with her head.
King: But she is only a child.
Queen: Well, do you play croquet?
Alice: Why, yes.
Queen: Well, come on then.
(King gives Alice a flamingo.)
Alice: But this is a flamingo and the balls are hedgehogs.
King: Well, how else will we play?
(Alice hits the ball and misses White Rabbit.)
White Rabbit: It is a fine day for a game of croquet.
Alice: Where is the Duchess?
White Rabbit: She has been sent to the High Tower. She is to be executed.
Alice: Why?
White Rabbit: Because she boxed the Queen's ears.
(Alice starts to laugh.)
White Rabbit: Hush, she will hear you.
Queen: Get to your places. Off with their heads! Off with their heads!
Cheshire Cat: How are you getting on?
Alice: Not very well; they are not playing fairly.
Cheshire Cat: How do you like the Queen?
Alice: She is not very nice, is she?
(There is a fanfare.)
White Rabbit: Quick, the trial is about to start.

Scene 8: The Trial

(The King and Queen sit on their thrones. Knave kneels before them.)

Knave: I am not guilty. I didn't do it.
King: Ace, read the charges.
Ace: The Queen of Hearts
She made some tarts,
All on a summer's day;
The Knave of Hearts
He stole those tarts.
King: Call the first witness.
Hatter: I haven't finished my tea.
King: Next witness. Give your evidence.
Cook: The tarts are made of treacle.
King: Call the next witness.
Ace: The next witness is Alice.
King: What do you know of this business?
Alice: Nothing.
King: Well, all the evidence points to knave being guilty.
Alice: No, it doesn't. It proves nothing of the sort.
Queen: Hold your tongue.
Alice: No, I won't. You are all nothing but a pack of cards.
Jury: Off with her head!

(Everyone rushes for Alice and the lights go off. Curtains close and Alice comes outside and sits on the steps. She is sleeping.)

Lorina: Alice, wake up, wake up, it is time to go home for tea. We are having treacle tart tonight.
Alice: *(Confused.)* It must have been a dream after all.

The following two plays, *How the Elephant Got His Trunk* and *How the Leopard Got His Spots* are based on two stories in the book *Just So Stories* by Rudyard Kipling.

About the Author:

Rudyard Kipling (1856-1936)

Rudyard Kipling was born on December 30, 1865, in Bombay, India. He was educated in England but he returned to India in 1882. He was considered one of the greatest British writers of his generation. Kipling's experiences in India formed the basis of stories. His short stories were compiled into an anthology of 40 short stories called *Plain Tales from the Hills.* This book became very popular in England. He moved to Vermont where he wrote *The Jungle Book (*1894), *The Naulahka: A Story of the West and East (1892)* and *The Second Jungle Book* (1895). By the age of 32, Kipling was the highest paid writer in the world. He received the Nobel Prize for Literature in 1907.

How the Elephant Got His Trunk

Characters: Three narrators, Elephant Child, Ostrich, Giraffe, Hippo, Python, Crocodile, Koloko Bird, Fly, Mother Elephant, Father Elephant

Narrator 1: Once upon a time, a long, long, time ago on the plains of Africa...
Narrator 2: ...there lived elephants who did not have any trunks.
Narrator 3: Instead, they had a little snout just like pigs have today. They couldn't drink through their snout.
Narrator 1: Nor could they pick up anything.
Narrator 2: There lived one elephant child who was very curious.
Narrator 3: He was always asking questions. He asked the Ostrich:
Elephant child: Ostrich, why do you bury your head?
Ostrich: I bury my head in the sand because I'm shy and don't like talking to people. Now, go away.
Elephant Child: Giraffe, why is your neck so long?
Giraffe: Because I'm very nosy and I like to see what his going on in the jungle.
Elephant Child: Hippo, why are your eyes so red?
Hippo: Because I swim in dirty water all day and it hurts my eyes.
Narrator 1: He asked questions about everything that he saw, smelt, felt, touched or tasted.
Narrator 2: One morning he had a new question that he had never asked before.
Elephant Child: I wonder what a crocodile has for dinner.
(All the animals tell him to be quiet and to stop asking such silly questions.)

Elephant Child: Fine. If you won't tell me, I'll ask the Koloko Bird. Koloko Bird, what does a crocodile have for dinner?
Koloko Bird: I don't know, but there is one way to find out.
Elephant Child: How?
Koloko Bird: Ask him.
Narrator 3: The next morning, Elephant Child set off to find out what crocodiles ate for dinner.
Elephant Child: Goodbye, everyone. I am going to the great, grey, green, greasy river to find out what crocodiles have for dinner.
Narrator 1: He came across a python.
Elephant Child: Excuse me, sir, but have you seen such a thing as a crocodile in these parts?
Python: Mmm, have I seen a crocodile? Let me see. *(He thinks for a few seconds.)* Why yes, if you keep going straight, you will arrive at the great, grey, green, greasy river.
Elephant Child: Thank you, Python. *(He arrives at the river.)* Excuse me. Have you seen a crocodile?
Crocodile: Why, I am a crocodile. Look, I can cry crocodile tears. *(He begins to cry.)* How can I help you?
Elephant Child: Well, I have come all this way to ask you what you have for dinner.
Crocodile: Come closer and I will tell you. *(Elephant Child moves closer.)* Closer, closer. (*He grabs Elephant Child by his nose.)* I think I will have an elephant's child for my dinner today.
Elephant Child: Let go of me. Help me, Python!
Narrator 1: Python pulled the elephant from behind.
Python: Koloko Bird, please help us. The Crocodile is trying to eat Elephant Child for his dinner.
Narrator 2: Python and Koloko Bird pulled the elephant from behind.
Koloko bird: Hippo, please help us. Crocodile is trying to eat Elephant Child for his dinner.

Narrator 3: Python, Koloko Bird and Hippo pulled the elephant from behind.
Hippo: Giraffe, please help us. Crocodile is trying to eat Elephant Child for his dinner.
Narrator 1: Python, Koloko Bird, Hippo and Giraffe pulled the elephant from behind.
Giraffe: Ostrich, please help us. Crocodile is trying to eat Elephant Child for his dinner.
Narrator 2: They all pulled the elephant from behind very hard and eventually Crocodile let go. *(They all fall on the ground and the crocodile swims off.)*
Elephant Child: Oh dear, look at my nose. It is all out of shape and it is way too long.
(A fly buzzes by and the elephant swats it with his trunk.)
Python: You couldn't have done that with your old nose.
Narrator 3: The elephant was hungry and he picked up some grass with his new nose.
Koloko Bird: You couldn't have done that with your old nose.
Narrator 3: Elephant Child was very hot and he sucked up water with his new nose and sprayed himself.
Hippo: You couldn't have done that with your old nose.
Narrator 1: Elephant Child went home to show off his new nose.
Mother Elephant: What did you do to your nose?
Elephant Child: I got a new nose from the crocodile on the banks of the great, grey, green, greasy river.
Narrator 2: He showed them all the new things he could do with his nose.
Father Elephant: How very useful. I want one of those.
Narrator 3: All the elephants saw how useful it was and one by one they went to the great, grey, green, greasy river to get new noses from the crocodile. The crocodile did a roaring trade until all the elephants in the jungle had long trunks like Elephant Child.
Crocodile: Roll up! Roll up! Get your new elephant noses here.

How the Leopard Got His Spots

Characters: Four narrators, the leopard, the giraffe, the hunter, the zebra, the eland, the wildebeest and Baviaan, the wise dog-headed baboon.

Narrator 1: Long, long ago. There lived a leopard who lived on the High Veldt.
Narrator 2: The High Veldt had lots of sand, sandy coloured rock and sandy yellowish grass.
Narrator 3: The giraffe, the zebra, the eland and the hartebeest also lived in the sandy coloured High Veldt.
Narrator 4: All the animals were a sandy yellowish brownish colour but the sandy yellowish brownish of them all was the leopard.
Narrator 1: The leopard was the same colour as the High Veldt to the letter.
Narrator 2: The other animals did not like this fact, as they could never see the leopard when he was hunting.
(The giraffe and zebra walk along and the leopard jumps up and scares them. He runs after them. Then, the eland and hartebeest walk by and the leopard jumps up and scares them. He chases the eland and the hartebeest.)
(Along comes a hunter. The hunter is the same colour as the leopard.)
Hunter: Leopard, you are just as sandy coloured and yellowish as me.
(They compare their skin colour.)
Leopard: We are the same colour as the High Veldt.
Hunter: I have an idea. Let's go hunting together. I will hunt with my bow and arrow.
Leopard: And I will hunt with my teeth and claws.
(They go hunting. The other animals run left and right across the stage a number of times. The hunter is on the

right side of the stage and the leopard is on the left side. Eventually, the chased animals are out of breath and they move to the centre of stage.)

Giraffe: What are we going to do?

Zebra: We can't roam peacefully on the High Veldt anymore because the hunter and the leopard are too difficult to spot.

Wildebeest: They are exactly the same colour as the high veldt.

Eland: I think it may be a good idea if we moved away.

Giraffe: Where would we go?

Zebra: I know a place; it is a great forest full of trees, bushes and striped, speckle, patchy, blotchy shadows.

Eland: What a good idea. They will never find us there.

Wildebeest: We will be able to live peacefully.

All animals: Let's go!

Narrator 3: All the animals moved away from the High Veldt.

Narrator 4: They scuttled for days and days until they came to the great forest.

Narrator 1: One day the zebra noticed that the giraffe's skin colour had changed.

Zebra: Giraffe, look how blotchy your skin has become.

Giraffe: Do you like it? My skin has become blotchy because I'm standing in out and of the shade all day.

Zebra: What do you think of my black and white stripes?

Eland and Wildebeest: Zebra, you look very nice. We have become darker with a little wavy lines on our back.

Giraffe: You look like the tree trunks.

Zebra: The leopard and the hunter would never find us here.

Narrator 2: Meanwhile on the High Veldt, the leopard and the hunter were getting very hungry.

Hunter: (*Looking around.)* Where have all the animals gone?

Narrator 3: They came across Baviaan, the barking dog-headed baboon.

Leopard: Let's ask Baviaan. He is the wisest animal in Africa.
Hunter: Where have all the animals gone?
Baviaan: The game have gone to the great big forest. My advice to you leopard is to change spots as soon as possible, and my advice to you hunter is just change.
Narrator 4: The hunter and the leopard were confused by the advice but they took off towards the forest.
Narrator 1: They travelled for days. They were about to give up when they saw the great big forest, full of tree trunks
Leopard: What is this place? It is so very dark but full of little pieces of light. (*They both looked around the forest in amazement.)*
Hunter: This just gets curiouser and curiouser. I can smell a giraffe and I can hear a giraffe but I can't see a giraffe.
Leopard: I can smell and zebra and I can hear a zebra but I can't see one.
(*The giraffe and the zebra are moving around the stage quietly; when the leopard or the hunter looks at them, they freeze.)*
Narrator 2: The hunter and the leopard waited until dark and pretended to sleep.
Narrator 3: The leopard heard something breathing heavily and he jumped on the noise.
(*The leopard jumps on the zebra and wrestles him to the ground. The zebra struggles but then stops.)*
Leopard: Be quite and stop struggling. I'm going to sit on your head until the morning and then I will see who you really are.
Narrator 4: From a distance, there was another crashing noise. The hunter had caught something else.
(Hunter captures the giraffe and wrestles him to the floor.)
Hunter: I caught something. It smells like a giraffe and feels like a giraffe but it doesn't have any form.

Leopard: Sit on its head until the morning and you will see its true form in the light.
Narrator 1: Morning came, eventually.
Leopard: What have you got at the end of the table, Brother?
(Hunter looks at the giraffe strangely and scratches his head.)
Hunter: It is most peculiar. It looks like a giraffe and smells like a giraffe but it is covered all over with brown blotches. What have you captured, Brother?
(Leopard looks at the zebra strangely and scratches his head.)
Leopard: Well, it looks like a zebra and smells like a zebra but it has these black and whites stripes all over its body. (*Looks at the zebra.)* Zebra, what have you being doing? Don't you know that if you were on the High Veldt, I would be able to see you for miles?
Zebra: We are not in the High Veldt now, Leopard.
Leopard: How did this happen?
Zebra: If you let us get up, we can show you.
Narrator 2: They let the giraffe and the zebra go. The zebra moved towards some bushes where the sunlight fell all in stripes and he disappeared. The giraffe moved towards some tall trees where he suddenly vanished.
Zebra and Giraffe: *(Laughing.)* Where's you breakfast, now?
Leopard: Where did they go?
Hunter: That is a clever trick. (*He looks at the leopard.)* Leopard, you could learn a lesson from them. You show up like a bar of soap in a coal bucket.
Leopard: Ha, ha. You can't talk. You show up in this forest like a mustard plaster on a sack of coals.
Hunter: Well, laughing at how silly we look won't catch breakfast. Remember what Baviaan told me. He said, I should change but I've nothing to change but my skin. I'm going to change my skin to blackish brown so I can hide behind trees and in hollows.

Narrator 3: The hunter changed his skin colour there and then.
Leopard: What about me?
Hunter: Take Baviaan's advice. He told you to go into spots. I'll dip my fingers in this paint and put spots all over your body.(*Hunter puts the tips of his fingers all over the leopard.)*
Leopard: You must make them small. I don't want to look like giraffe.
Hunter: You look beautiful. Now, you can lie on rocks and look like a piece of stone or lie on a tree and look like sunshine shifting through the leaves.
Leopard: Let's go find some breakfast.
Narrator 4: And off they went into the deep forest and lived happily ever after, and they were never hungry again.

The following three plays are based on stories in Oscar Wilde's book *The Happy Prince and Other Tales*.

About the Author:

Oscar Wilde (1854-1900)

Oscar Wilde was born on October 16, 1854, in Dublin. He was a novelist and a playwright. He is most famous for his novel *The Picture of Dorian Grey* (1891) and his play *The Importance of Being Earnest* (1895). This two pieces of work are considered to be amongst the great literary masterpieces of the Victorian era. Wilde died of meningitis in 1900. He was only 46 years old.

The Happy Prince

Characters: Grandad, two grandchildren, three town councillors, Mother, Little Boy, Swallow, five swallows, Young Writer, Teacher, two schoolchildren, Match Girl, Melter

Child 1: We are bored. Granddad, wake up.
Child 2: Wake up, Granddad. We are bored; we have played with all our toys and we have nothing else to do.
Child 1: Granddad, will you tell us one of your stories?
Granddad: Of course I will. Children, come over here and sit down. Have I told you the story of the Happy Prince?
Children: No.
Granddad: Well, long, long time ago, high above the city, there stood the most beautiful statue. It was the statue of the Happy Prince.
Child 1: What did he look like?
Granddad: He was covered all over with fine gold. He had two bright sapphires for his eyes and a large red ruby glowed on the top of his sword.*(Statue is standing centre stage, very still.)*
Town Councillor: (*Looks up at the statue with admiration.)* He is as beautiful as a weathercock. Unfortunately he is not very useful during these hard times. *(Mother and Little Boy enter; Little Boy is crying.)*
Mother: Why are you crying?
Little boy: Because I want to go to the moon.
Mother: Why can't you be like the Happy Prince? He never dreams of crying for anything.
Town Councillor: I'm glad there is someone in this city that is happy.
(They walk off.)
(Enter some school children and their teacher.)
School child 1: *(Looks up at the statue.)* He looks like an angel.

Teacher: How do you know what an angel looks like?
School child 2: We have seen them in our dreams.
Teacher: Don't be ridiculous. Everybody knows children don't dream.
(Six swallows come flying in and land near the statue.)
Swallow 1: It is getting cold now.
Swallow 2: We should go to warmer climes.
Swallow 3: I was thinking of Florida.
Swallow 4: We can't go to Florida, as there are lots of hurricanes there.
Swallow 5: I have a good idea. Let's go to Egypt.
Swallow: I can't go. (*Looks like he is in love.)*
Swallow 1: Why ever not?
Swallow 2: You will freeze if you stay here.
Swallow: You know, I have fallen in love with the most beautiful reed I have ever seen.
Swallow 3: Oh how romantic. Please tell us how you met. I love romantic stories.
Swallow: Well, I was chasing a yellow moth down by the river and there she was...
(Re-enacts the scene.)
Swallow: Oh my! You are the most beautiful reed I have ever seen.
Reed: Why thank you, Mr. Swallow.
Swallow: I shall love you forever.
Reed: Why, of course!
Grandad: The reed made him a low bow so he flew around her, touching the water with his wings and making silver ripples. This romance lasted through the summer.
Swallow 4: This is ridiculous.
Swallow 5: She has no money and too many cousins.
Swallow 3: I think it is romantic.
Swallow 1: Well we are off. Are you coming or not?
Swallow 2: Ask her to come with you because you can't stay here.
(Swallow flies to the river and sees the reed.)
Swallow: Reed, will you come to Egypt with me?
Reed: Of course not. My home is here with my cousins.

Swallow: You have been playing with my feelings. I'm off to find my friends and we are going to the pyramids.
(Swallow flies off.)
Grandad: By the time he reached the city, it was night and his friends had gone. He took shelter on the feet of the Happy Prince statue. As he was just about to fall asleep, a drop of water fell on him.
Swallow: How strange. There is not a single cloud in the sky, the stars are clear and bright and yet it is raining.
(Another drop falls.)
Swallow: What a useless statue; it can't keep the rain off. It is not rain, it is the statue. He is crying. Why are you crying, Happy Prince?
Happy Prince: When I was alive and had a human heart, I played all day in the palace and I never cared what happened outside the palace. I lived such a happy life, but now I'm dead and I'm up here. I can see all the misery and hardship in my city.
Swallow: What can I do to help?
Happy Prince: Take the ruby from my sword and give it to the woman whose son has a fever and who can't afford oranges.
Woman: What can I do to make it better?
Little Boy: I want some oranges.
Woman: We can't afford them.
(Swallow drops off the ruby and the woman finds it.)
Woman: Maybe we can afford oranges after all.
(Swallow returns to the Happy Prince.)
Swallow: I must go to Egypt to be with my friends.
Happy Prince: Just stay one more day and be my messenger. I see a young man in a small room. He is trying to finish a play for the director of the theatre, but he is too cold to write. He has fainted from hunger. Pluck out one of my eyes and give it to him so he can sell it to the jeweller and buy food and firewood and finish his play.
Swallow: I can't do that.
Happy Prince: Do as I command you.

(The swallow drops the sapphire off in the young man's room.)
Young writer: I am beginning to be appreciated; this must be from a great admirer.
(Swallow has returned to the statue.)
Swallow: I've come to say goodbye.
Happy Prince: Swallow, Swallow, will you not stay one more night? I need your help. In the square is a little Match Girl. She has dropped her matches and her father will beat her. Pluck out my other eye and give it to her.
(Swallow drops the sapphire in front of the Match Girl.)
Match Girl: Oh what a beautiful stone. *(She runs home laughing.)*
Swallow: You are blind now so I will stay with you always.
Happy Prince: No, little Swallow. You must got to Egypt to be with your friends in the warm climate.
Swallow: I will stay with you always. *(Falls asleep at the prince's feet.)*
Happy Prince: I'm covered with fine gold. You must take it off, leaf by leaf, and give it to the poor.
Granddad: The swallow did just that—leaf after leaf of fine gold he gave to the poor. The children's faces grew rosier and rosier and they laughed and played games. The winter came and the swallow grew colder and colder, but he would not leave the prince. He knew he was going to die.
Swallow: Goodbye, dear Prince. Will you let me kiss your hand?
Happy Prince: I'm glad you are going to Egypt at last. You must kiss me on the lips for I love you.
Swallow: I am not going to Egypt but to the house of death.
(Swallow kisses the prince and falls down dead at his feet.)
Granddad: Just then there was an almighty crack from inside the statue. His lead heart had snapped in two.

Town Councillor: The statue looks very shabby, and look at this dead bird at his feet. *(Points to the dead swallow.)* We must issue a law that birds are no longer allowed to die. We need to take down the statue. He is no longer beautiful.
Granddad: They then melted the statue down.
Melter: What a strange thing—this broken heart will not melt in the furnace. I will throw it away.
(He throws it into the rubbish bin next to where the dead bird was laying.)

The Selfish Giant

Characters: The Selfish Giant; The Cornish Ogre; 3 parts of the wall: Sad, Lazy and Frightened; 2 Trees; Ice; Frost; Snow; Wind; Narrator/Old man; 8 Children: Anna/Billy/Cathy/Ger/Dick/Ellie/Fred/Harry; 2 grandchildren.

(Curtains are closed. The opening scene is an old man sitting with his two grandchildren grouped around him, sitting downstage left. Selfish Giant and Cornish Ogre are sitting centre stage, miming drinking tea and talking.)

Narrator/Old man: Children come over here and I will tell you the story of a giant that lived a long time ago. He had a lovely, beautiful garden with soft, green grass. There were the most amazing flowers and twelve fabulous peach trees. However, the giant was very selfish, and he shared his garden with no one.

Old Man: He used to say...

Selfish Giant: My own garden is my own garden and no one else can use it!

Old Man: The giant had been to visit his friend the Cornish Ogre and stayed seven years.

(Giant and Ogre drink tea and mime having a conversation.)

Selfish Giant: I have been here for seven years, and we have run out of things to talk about.

Cornish Ogre: Yes, you have been here a long time, so maybe it is time you went back to your beautiful, empty garden.

Old Man: They said goodbye and the Selfish Giant returned home.

(Giant waves goodbye and they both leave the stage, going in different directions.)

Old Man: However, what the Selfish Giant didn't know was that his garden was being used by the local school children.
(School bell rings. Eight children run up the centre aisle and start to play with the children in the audience. They run down the side aisles and reach the steps to the stage. The curtains open and there is a wall, centre stage, with three parts to it. There is the happy part of the wall; a frightened part of the wall; and a lazy part of the wall. The lazy part is in the centre. There are also two trees on each side of the stage: centre stage left and centre stage right. The children squeeze through a hole in the wall.)
Anna: Right, I've got through! Come on, Cathy. I'll give you a hand. Mind the nettles.
Billy: Ouch! Take care, Cathy, the nettles are very bad today. Watch out.
Cathy: All right. Nearly through. *(She pushes her way in.)* That's it. Here at last. (*Sighing.)* Wonderful!
(Children chat as four more go through the hole, one-by-one.)
Dick: (*The last one is trying to get through but has difficulty.)* This hole seems to be getting smaller and smaller, unless it's my imagination.
Ellie: No, you've got that wrong, Dick. You're getting fatter. It's all that fast food you eat.
(Children all laugh and pull Dick through the hole.)
Ger: I love this place so much, and I am so happy when we are all in here playing.
(Everyone agrees by nodding their heads.)
Harry: It's been seven years since the giant was here. I know it's his garden, but he can't come back after all this time, can he?
Fred: I hope not. But just in case, we'd better make the most of it while we've got it.
(Children go off-stage. Lights focus on the three parts of the wall.)
Frightened: Wake up, Lazy. If the Selfish Giant comes back, we will be in trouble.

Lazy: The giant hasn't been here for seven years. I am tired of holding up the centre of the wall.
Happy: I love seeing all the children playing in the garden. I am so happy when they come into the garden, but, Lazy, I think you should wake-up.
Lazy: I am going back to sleep. *(Starts snoring.)*
Frightened: I'm scared. I have a bad feeling.
Happy: You are always scared. Try to cheer up and be happy that the sun is shining and the children are having such a good time playing in the garden.
Tree 1: Lazy needs to wakeup.
Tree 2: Why don't we ask the audience to help us?
Tree 1: That's a good idea. When we count to three, everyone must say, "Wake-up, Lazy."
Happy, Frightened and the trees: One, two, three audience, everybody together: Wake-up, Lazy.
(Eight Children come back on the stage and the trees and the two parts of the wall freeze.)
Fred: Let's play a game of Stuck in the Mud!
Ger: No, that's really boring.
Ellie: I know! Let's play Giant's Footsteps.
Billy: That's not funny.
Dick: What about Blind Man's Bluff?
All: Oh yes!
Cathy: Here's my tie. Come on, Fred. Ready for the blindfold?
Fred: I'm not doing it.
Anna: You are a scaredy-cat.
All except Fred and Harry: Scaredy-cat; scaredy-cat.
Harry: Leave him alone, I will do it.
(Harry is blindfolded and the game begins. They run around having fun. There is the sound of footsteps.)
Tree 1: Did you hear that?
Tree 2: Hear what?
Frightened: I heard it too. Wake up, Lazy.
Lazy: I'm sleeping.
(Giant enters while the children are playing.)
Happy: Lazy, I think you need to wake up. NOW!

(All the children see the giant and they begin to squirm and then all run away.)
Giant: How on earth did those horrible children get inside my garden?
(Looks at the wall and sees Lazy only half-standing up.)
Giant: I see where the problem is. Lazy, wakeup now!
(Lazy jumps up and stands at attention.)
Frightened: *(Whispers.)* I told you he was going to come back.
Giant: Wall, if you don't stand up properly, I am going to knock you down and build a new, stronger wall. This is my garden and NO ONE is allowed in here. I know what I'm going to do. I'm going to put up a sign.
(Giant gets a sign and puts it around Lazy's neck.)
Giant: *(Shouts at the children.)* Can you read this sign, you horrible children?
Children: Trespassers will be persecuted.
Giant: No, you ignorant children. It is TRESPASSERS will be PROSECUTED.
Lazy: What does that mean?
Happy: It means anyone will be in trouble if they come into the garden.
(Giant exits, muttering. Curtains close to change the scene.)
Narrator/Old Man: Now the children had nowhere to play.
(Curtains open. The stage has changed, as the trees are now behind the wall and they are all upstage to give the illusion that the children are outside the garden.)
Anna: Why does the giant have to be so mean?
Billy: We have nowhere to play now.
Cathy: We weren't doing him any harm.
Dick: Where will we play now?
Ellie: The road!
Fred: We could get knocked down.
Ger: We have no choice now.
(The children look forlorn and play with their heads down. They all look toward the garden.)

Harry: How happy we were there!
(The children slowly walk off the stage.)
Narrator/Old Man: Spring came over the country. There were flowers blooming, trees in blossom and birds singing. Only in the garden of the selfish giant it was still winter. The birds did not care to sing in it as there were no children. And the flowers had no heart to bloom.
Ice: Well, Frost, I think our work has been done here.
Frost: I'm looking forward to having a break.
(Ice suddenly notices the sign: "Trespassers will be prosecuted.")
Ice: Look at this.
Frost: That Selfish Giant won't share his garden.
Ice: I know. Let's stay here until the Selfish Giant learns to share his beautiful garden.
Frost: I know, I will call Wind and Snow and get them to come and help. (*Takes out a mobile phone and rings them. Wind shows up immediately.)*
Wind: What's the big emergency? I was very busy in Florida. It is hurricane season, you know.
Ice: Wait until Snow gets here and we will tell you all about it.
(A few seconds later, Snow arrives onstage.)
Snow: I'm here.
Wind: What took you so long?
Snow: I was in Lapland helping Santa. What's the big emergency?
Frost: Anyway, look at this sign. The Selfish Giant won't share his garden, so we are going to stay here until he changes his mind.
(Ice, Frost, Wind and Snow freeze. Giant enters stage left, looking sad.)
Narrator/Old Man: The giant was very sad. A year passed and he began to realise he was very selfish. One day he saw one of the children under a tree crying and he went to help him.
(Giant mimes seeing the child. Nobody else can see him.)

Giant: Please, let me help. *(He reaches under the tree and mimes lifting up a child.)* I have been a very selfish giant. I will open my garden up to everyone. *(He takes down the sign and exits.)*
Ice: Frost, I think he has learned his lesson.
Frost: It's time to go. I heard there is an ogre in Cornwall who hasn't been very nice.
Ice: Wind and Snow, come on. It is time to go.
Snow: Do you have a map?
Frost: No! But I have my new Sat Nav/GPS.
Ice: Come on, let's go!
(They leave the stage. One of the children spies a hole in the wall and climbs through. He calls the others.)
Fred: I can't believe we are inside the garden again!
Dick: It's spring time.
Billy: Winter has gone.
Cathy: And there's no notice. The giant's notice is gone!
Harry: And the garden is more beautiful than ever.
(The children hear the giant's footsteps and hide behind the trees. Giant comes onstage and sees them. He waves them over. They are frightened but they move towards him slowly.)
Giant: Now I would like to join your games, if you please! (*Suddenly looking around.)* But where is your little friend?
Anna: What are you talking about, sir?
Billy: Do you mean Fred over there?
Fred: He doesn't mean me. He means Dick. (*He pushes Dick forward.)*
Dick: Did you want something *(stuttering nervously),* Mmmmister...ssssir...Mmmister ... Fffffriendly...Giant?
Giant: I want to know where the little boy is, the one that I lifted up into the branches of the tree.
Ellie: But we haven't been in the garden since you put the sign up. Well not until today.
Fred: Then we heard your footsteps.
Anna: So we hid by the wall. I'm sorry that we trespassed in your garden, Mr. Giant.

(All apologize, suddenly worried that the giant might become selfish again.)

Giant: Oh no, no, no. You don't need to say sorry. I am the one who is sorry. Please think of this garden as yours now. But I wish you could tell me where the little child lives. I am very fond of him because it is through him that I realised I had been selfish with my garden. No wonder spring never came!

Ger: But this is all of us. No one else came with us.

Billy: But we will ask around in school tomorrow and see if we can find out about your little friend.

Giant: Oh, yes, please. Now I really must have my rest. My old bones ache from all the playing. You carry on playing.

(Giant sits on the side of the stage and the children continue to play in slow motion.)

Narrator/Old Man: The years passed but the children were never able to find out who the giant's little friend had been. The giant grew very, very old. He could no longer play, so he sat in a huge armchair and watched the children. They all feared he would die soon.

(Giant mimes seeing the small child and calls out to him. Only Giant can see the small child. The children all stop playing immediately when they hear Giant talking. They look around but they can't see anyone.)

Giant: There he is! Come on, little friend. Where have you been? I've waited so long for you. Come and join in the fun. *(He hobbles towards the child.)* My goodness, how I've missed you! I had a feeling I might die before you came to see me again. *(Giant moves to hug the child, and then draws back in horror as he takes the child's hands and examines them.)*

Giant: Why, who has dared wound you? Tell me quickly, and I'll fetch my sword and kill him.

Small Child: *(Audience just hears the voice, they don't see small child; the voice can be done by the teacher or drama facilitator.)* No, these are the wounds of love.

Giant: *(Suddenly in awe.)* Who are you?

Small Child: Once you let me play in your garden. Today, you shall come with me to a very special garden called Paradise.
(Giant sinks slowly to the ground. The small child kneels beside the giant, makes him comfortable and comforts him. The children, aware Giant has died, sadly gather flowers and places them around him.)

The Canterville Ghost

Characters: Lord Canterville, Mr Otis, Mrs Otis, Virginia, James, Lewis, Clark, (Lewis and Clark are twins), Mrs Umney and Sir Simon (the ghost).
(Outside Canterville Castle there is a sign for sale which Lord Canterville is taking down.)

Scene 1: Canterville Castle
Lord Canterville: Well, it looks like we have a deal, Mr Otis. The castle is yours.
Mr Otis: Thank you, Lord Canterville. I'm sure my family will be very happy here.*(They shake hands.)*
Lord Canterville: *(Looks at him hesitantly.)* Perhaps, I should mention that Canterville Castle is haunted by a ghost. (*Ghost walks in behind them. They don't see the ghost but the audience does.)*
Mr. Otis: I don't believe in ghosts, Lord Canterville, so I'm sure I have nothing to be frightened of. (*They exit the stage.)*
(Mr and Mrs Otis and their four children, Virginia, James, Lewis and Clark, enter. They are greeted by an old woman dressed in an apron.)
Mrs Umney: Welcome, I'm Mrs Umney the housekeeper. Please, come in. There is tea in the library. *(There is a table and two chairs on the left side of the stage. Mr and Mrs Otis sit on them and Mrs Umney serves them tea.)*
Virginia: It is so exciting.
James: I know, let's explore. *(The four children run around the stage. They mime opening and closing doors.)*
Lewis: Look what's that? *(He picks a note up from the floor.)*
Clark: It's a note.
Virginia: Let me see.

James: If a child enters the secret room and stays until dead of night.
Lewis: Then at last Sir Simon can sleep in his tomb and at Canterville all will be alright.
Clark: What does that mean?
(Meanwhile in the library Mrs Otis is inspecting the ground carefully.)
Mrs Otis: I'm terribly sorry, Mrs Umney. I think I spilled something on your carpet.
Mrs Umney: That's not tea, it is blood.
Mr Otis: We must get rid of it. *(The children all come in and inspect the blood stain on the carpet.)*
Mrs Umney: I'm afraid that is impossible. That is the blood of Lady Eleanor Canterville. She was murdered by her husband Sir Simon Canterville 500 years ago. Then, Sir Simon disappeared and his body has never been found. They say his spirit haunts the house.
Lewis: I'll get rid of it. *(He rubs it.)*
Clark: Look it's gone.
(Then there is thunder and lightning and Mrs Umney faints. Lights go out. When the lights come back on, the blood stain is back.)
Mr Otis: Maybe the house is haunted after all.

Scene 2: Night-time in the Castle
(Mr and Mrs Otis are asleep in bed. There is a strange ratting noise and it was getting louder and louder. Mr Otis gets up and puts on his slippers and dressing gown. He opens the door and there in front is the ghost in chains.)
Mr Otis: Oh, you must be Sir Simon.
Sir Simon: *(Nods.)* Yes I am. (*He rattles his chains really loudly.)*
Mr. Otis: Here, take this bottle of oil (*he hands the bottle to the ghost)* and oil your chains. They are making too much noise. I can't sleep.
(*Sir Simon throws the bottle on the ground and runs away and starts to make haunting noise.)*

(The two twins come on stage rubbing their eyes.)
Lewis: What's going on?
Clark: Who is making all that noise? *(They stop and share at the ghost.)*
Lewis: It's the ghost.
Clark: Here, throw your pillow at him to scare him (*They throw the pillows and run off stage.)*
Sir Simon: Well, I never. I have been scaring people for nearly 500 years and I have never been treated like this. Don't worry, I will get my revenge.

Scene 3: The Next Morning.
(Family are sitting at the table for breakfast.)
Mrs Otis: Children, you mustn't be frightened of the ghost.
Mr. Otis: Well, he didn't look very scary to me. (*Sir Simon comes out from the other side of the stage and stares at the family.)*
Sir Simon: I will exact my revenge on those pesky children.
(The following is all done through mime. The children dress up as ghosts and scare Sir Simon. They hold a piece of string and trip him up. They put oil on the floor and he slips. They run off laughing. This can be done with music in the background.)
Sir Simon: I'll stop those children once and for all. I'll appear as my most terrifying characters Reckless Rupert. Reckless Rupert always scares people. (*He tiptoes into the children's room and a bucket of water is thrown on him. The children laugh and he goes off dejected.)*
Lewis: We haven't seen the ghost for ages.
Clark: I think maybe we scared in off for good.
(They exit the stage.)
(Ghost comes in and sits on a chair. He is crying. Virginia walks in.)
Virginia: Why are you crying, Sir Simon? *(She puts her arm around his shoulder to comfort him.)*

Sir Simon: Because your brothers keep playing nasty tricks on me.
Virginia: They would stop if you behaved yourself.
Sir Simon: But I'm a ghost. I have to rattle my chains and moan and groan and walk around at night.
Virginia: You have been wicked. You murdered your wife. It's wrong to kill people.
Sir Simon: I know but her brother captured me and starved me to death.
Virginia: You poor ghost.
Sir Simon: Please help me. I'm so unhappy and so very tired.
Virginia: Have you not slept?
Sir Simon: I haven't slept for 500 years.
Virginia: I don't know how I can help.
Sir Simon: You could. Do you remember the note you found?
Virginia: *(Takes it out of her pocket and reads it.)* But I don't know what it means.
Sir Simon: It means that you must come with me to my chamber and pray for me.
Virginia: That sound easy enough.
Sir Simon: No person has ever entered the chamber and come out alive.
Virginia: I'll come with you.
(Off they go and disappear.)
(Mrs Otis and the other children come on stage looking for Virginia.)
Mrs Otis: Where is she?
Mr Otis: I'm getting worried.
(Then they hear a crash and she comes out of the secret chamber.)
Mrs Otis: Where have you been?
Virginia: I've been with the ghost. He knows he has been wicked and he is very sorry for everything. He gave me this box of jewels.*(They all look at the expensive jewels.)*

Final scene: At the Graveyard

(There is a gravestone that's says "Sir Simon Canterville RIP." The whole family, Mrs. Umney and Lord Canterville all walk in and bow their heads in respect.)
Lord Canterville: Finally he is at peace.
Virginia: He is happy at last.

The next play is based on the book *Peter Pan* by J.M Barrie.

About the Author:

J.M Barrie (1860-1937)

J.M Barrie was born on May 9, 1860, in Forfarshire, Scotland. Barrie worked as a journalist before he published his first novel *Better Dead* in 1887. He is best known for the children's book *Peter Pan* (1904) and *The Boy Who Would Never Grow up* (1916). Barrie died in 1937 and he bequeathed the copyright of Peter Pan to a children's hospital. Disney released the animated cartoon classic *Peter Pan* in 1953.

Peter Pan

Characters: Two storytellers, Wendy, John, Michael, Peter Pan, Tinkerbelle, four lost boys, Captain Hook, Crocodile, Tigerlilly, Mister Smee, two pirates and Mrs. Darling.

Storyteller 1: Deep in the heart of London where the Darling family lived, Wendy Darling shared a nursery with her two brothers John and Michael. At bedtime she would tell her brothers about a faraway place called Neverland.
(Centre stage, Wendy, John and Michael are fast asleep.)
Wendy: *(Wakes up and rubs her eyes.)* Oh! Peter Pan I'm so delighted to see you.
Peter Pan: My shadow escaped last night. Tinkerbelle and I are searching for it. Would you like to help me find it? *(Tinkerbelle is behind Peter on the stage left and she doesn't look happy. She makes a face behind Wendy's back.)*
Wendy: I will help you look for your shadow but only if my two younger brothers, John and Michael, can come with us. (*She points to them sleeping on the stage.)*
Peter Pan: Of course they can come. Fly with me to Neverland and you will never grow up there. Think happy thoughts. (*They wake John and Michael who look tired and confused.)*
Storyteller 2: Tinkerbelle sprinkles magic pixie dust over all of them so they can fly. Before they knew it the children were flying above the rooftops of London. As they fly to Neverland, Tinkerbelle get jealous of Wendy and flies ahead. When they arrive in Neverland, they meet the lost boys.
Peter Pan: *(Makes appropriate introductions.)*May, I introduce you to the Lost Boys. *(They all hug and shake hands.)* Boys, will you, John and Michael go capture some Indians while I show Wendy around Neverland?

Storyteller 1: While Peter was showing Wendy around, they see something unusual in the distance.

Peter Pan: Why, look! It's Captain Hook. (*They follow Captain Hook to Skull Island and sneak up behind him. Captain Hook and his crocodile have Tigerlilly tied up.)*

Captain Hook: If you don't tell me where Peter's Pan's hideout is, I will leave you here by the rocks to drown.

Tigerlilly: I will never tell you where to find Peter Pan. *(Peter flies down in front of the captain.).*

Captain Hook: Peter Pan, at last I found you.

Storyteller 2: Peter Pan and Captain Hook have a sword fight. The captain slips and Mr. Smee, the Captain's most trusted pirate, catches him in the boat. Peter and Wendy free Tigerlilly and they all fly back to Peter Pan's secret hideout.

Storyteller 1: Meanwhile back in Captain Hook's ship he hatches an evil plan.

Captain Hook: Mister Smee! I hear Tinkerbelle is cross with Peter. Go bring her to me.

Mister Smee: Aye, aye, Captain.

(Mister Smee finds Tinkerbelle and brings her willingly to talk to Captain Hook.)

Captain Hook: Show me where Peter Pan's secret hideout is.

Tinkerbelle: I will show you only if you promise not to harm Peter! *(She points out where Peter's hideout on the map.)*

Captain Hook: *(Grabs Tinkerbelle and locks her in a glass lantern.)* At last, I will get my revenge on Peter Pan.

Storyteller 2: Meanwhile back in Peter's hideout, Wendy, John and Michael were feeling homesick, but little did they know that Captain Hook had set a trap for them outside Peter Pan's secret hideout.

Michael and John: *(Sobbing.)* We want to go home.

Wendy: We shall go home. (*She looks at the lost boys.)* Do you boys want to come with us?

Lost Boys: Oh yes, please!

Wendy: Goodbye Peter. I will never forget you. (*She waves goodbye to Peter and walks away with the boys.)*
Captain Hook and the pirates: AHA! Got you! (*Captain Hook, Mister Smee and the pirates ambush the boys and Wendy. They take them to their ship, where they tie them up. Captain Hook leaves a present for Peter.)*
Storyteller 1: Captain Hook left a present for Peter Pan with a label that said, "To Peter, with love from Wendy." Meanwhile back at the ship....
Captain Hook: You have a choice: Either sign your name in my pirate book and join my pirate gang or walk the plank.
Wendy: We will never join your pirate gang; Peter Pan will save us.
Captain Hook: Not this time, my dear. A bomb very soon he will be blown out of Neverland forever! *(He laughs loudly.)* Ha, ha, ha.
Storyteller 2: Tinkerbelle breaks free from her lantern and flies desperately to the hideout to warn Peter. Peter was just about to open the present when Tinkerbelle grabs it from him and throws it as far as she can. *Booooommmm.* (*They take cover.)*
Tinkerbelle: Peter, Captain Hook has captured everybody and will make them walk the plank if they don't join his pirate gang.
Peter: Oh no! Let's go save them. *(Peter and Tinkerbelle go to the rescue.)*
Captain Hook: *(Surprised.)* Arhhhhhhhhh! We meet again, lad. This time I will finish you.
Peter Pan: Not on your life!
Storyteller 1: Peter Pan and Captain Hook have another sword fight. Captain Hook loses his balance, slips and falls backwards and is chased by a crocodile. Captain Hook tries to swim to the boat with the crocodile close behind.
(Everybody points at Captain Hook and laughs.)
Wendy: Peter, we really do have to go. I hope you find your shadow. (*Looks at the Lost Boys.)* Boys, are you coming?

Lost Boys: No, we are going to stay here and help Peter Pan look for his shadow and fight against the Evil Captain Hook.

(They all hug.)

Storyteller 2: The next morning....

(Wendy, John and Michael are sleeping centre stage and Mrs. Darling enters.)

Mrs. Darling: Morning children, time to wake up.

(Children wake up and run to her and give her a great big hug.)

Children: We are so happy to see you.

Mrs. Darling: *(Looks confused.)* I'm very happy to see you too.

The next play is based on *The Adventures of Pinocchio* by Carlo Collodi.

About the Author:

Carlo Collodi (1826-1890)

Carlo Collodi was the nom de plume of Carlo Lorenzini. Lorenzini was born on November 24, 1826, in the Grand Duchy of Tuscany. His writing career started with the publication of reviews submitted to various journals. *The Adventures of Pinocchio* was first serialised in a children's magazines from 1881 to1883. Due to its popularity, Pinocchio was turned into a novel, which instantly became a children's bestseller. Lorenzini died in Florence on 26 October 1890.

Pinocchio

Characters: Three narrators, Geppetto, Pinocchio, the cricket, the blue fairy, four puppets, fire eater, cat, fox, Lampwick, five children.

Narrator 1: Our story begins one night in the workshop of old Geppetto the carpenter. Geppetto decides to make a puppet out of a piece of wood. He took a lot time carving the puppet. When he eventually finished, it looked real.
Geppetto: *(Admires his puppet.)* I wish I had a real son; you are only made of wood. What shall I call you? Mmmmm. If I had a real son, I would call him Pinocchio, so I will call you Pinocchio. Good night, Pinocchio. Sleep well.
Narrator 2: Later that night, the Blue Fairy flew into the workshop. She saw the puppet and touched it with her wand.
Blue Fairy: Wake up, Pinocchio, and be a good son to old Geppetto. If you are kind and helpful, perhaps one day would will become a real boy.
Pinocchio: I will try to be as helpful as I can and help my father Geppetto as much as I can.
Blue Fairy: This is the cricket. He will be your friend. Listen to him carefully.
Narrator 3: But Pinocchio took no notice of the cricket. He was very naughty and was always getting into trouble.
Narrator 1: Geppetto wanted Pinocchio to have a good education, so he sells his coat to buy books for his new son.
Geppetto: Here are your books, Pinocchio. Now off you go to school and remember to listen to your teachers.
Pinocchio: Goodbye, father. I will try my hardest to be good.
Narrator 2: Pinocchio and the cricket set off but they only walked a short distance when they hear music coming from a theatre.

Pinocchio: Come on, Cricket. Let's see what is happening in there. It sounds exciting.
Cricket: No, Pinocchio, you must go to school instead. Hurry up or we will be late.
Narrator 3: Pinocchio ignores the cricket's advice and exchanges his school book for a ticket to the puppet show.
Cricket: Come back, Pinocchio!
Narrator 1: Pinocchio enters the theatre and is surprised to see lots of wooden puppets but, unlike him, they have strings to make them move.
Puppet 1: Look at the little wooden puppet.
Puppet 2: What's your name?
Puppet 3: Where have you come from?
Puppet 4: But where are your strings?
Puppet 5: You are welcome to join us but the fire eater, our master, is very cruel. If the puppet shows don't make enough money, he gets angry and throws one of us into the fire to heat his supper.
Fire Eater: What's all this noise? Why are you puppets talking instead of working? Talking doesn't pay the bills. Now, who wants to feel the heat of the fire? Hello, who's this? A puppet without strings! Come here young man; people will pay lots of money to see you.
Narrator 1: Fire eater grabs Pinocchio and locks him in a cage. He and the rest of the puppets then leave for the next show.
Pinocchio: Oh Cricket, why didn't I listen to you and got to school? What am I going to do now? How can I get out of the cage?
Narrator 2: Pinocchio starts to cry. Suddenly, the blue fairy appears and asks Pinocchio why he is locked in the cage. He tells her how foolish he has been.
Blue Fairy: Pinocchio, I will release you this time but you must promise to go straight home to your poor father.
Blue Fairy: Here are five pieces of gold so Geppetto can buy a new coat for himself and new school books for you. Keep the gold safe, Pinocchio.
Pinocchio: I promise to go straight home, Blue Fairy.

Narrator 3: Pinocchio sets off home and with his god coins in his hands. After a short distance, he meets a lame fox and blind cat.

Pinocchio: I must them of my good fortune, so they can share my happiness.

Cricket: What did you promise the Blue Fairy?

Pinocchio: But they seem so friendly. What harm can it do? Hello you two, look at these 5 gold coins I am taking home to my father.

Cat: How would like to make twice that much money?

Fox: Just think how happy your father would be if you brought back 10 gold coins instead of five.

Cat: Meet us at the inn tonight and will show you how to get rich.

Cricket: Don't listen to them, Pinocchio. They will trick you. Come on home now.

Narrator 3: Pinocchio didn't listen to Cricket and instead made his way to the inn. As it begins to get dark, he hears strange noises and sees two men following him.

Pinocchio: I'll hide my gold coins in my mouth for safe keeping.

Narrator 3: The robbers catch Pinocchio, but they can't get him to open his mouth so they leave him tied to a tree feeling sorry for himself. A raven tells the Blue Fairy where Pinocchio is and she comes to rescue him once more.

Blue Fairy: Why are you tied to this tree, Pinocchio? Why are you not at home with your father like you promised?

Pinocchio: Oh Blue Fairy, I had my gold coins stolen and then I got lost in the forest and fell down a ditch.

Narrator 1: Every time Pinocchio tells a lie, his nose gets longer and longer. He begins to cry again.

Blue Fairy: See Pinocchio, a liar is always found out but I shall forgive you this time. Now go straight home and don't talk to anyone.

Narrator 2: Pinocchio and the cricket arrive at Geppetto's house to find it empty. A note tells him he has gone looking for his son, Pinocchio.

Narrator 3: Pinocchio decides to stay at home and wait for his father but he is soon distracted again by Lampwick, the laziest boy in school.
Lampwick: Pinocchio, why do you study so hard? You could have fun all day if you come with me to Pleasure Island.
Cricket: Pinocchio wants to please his father, Geppetto, by showing him he isn't naughty anymore. Don't you, Pinocchio?
Narrator 1: But Pinocchio is always getting bored with being good. One night, he joins Lampwick and runs away to Pleasure Island. There are no adults or schools there so children can do exactly what they like and enjoy themselves all day and all night as well.
Narrator 2: Pinocchio and Lampwick have a great time doing all the things they know their parents would disapprove of. All goes well until one day they look at each other and see...
Pinocchio and Lampwick: Donkey's ears
Lampwick: Look Pinocchio, all the other children are donkeys too.
Child 1: Help! I've got a tail.
Child 2: I can't stand up anymore.
Child 3/4/5: What is happening to us?
Pinocchio: Cricket, Cricket, look at us! Why is this happening?
Cricket: All children who refuse to learn in school turn into donkeys in the end. It's no good I've tried my best to advise you but you never listen to me so I'm off. Goodbye Pinocchio and good luck.
Narrator 1: Pinocchio and some of the donkeys are taken away to be sold at the market. Pinocchio escapes by jumping into the sea where he becomes a puppet once more. But poor Pinocchio's troubles aren't yet for as he swims to freedom. He is swallowed by Monstrous the whale.

Narrator 2: Pinocchio tumbles down the whale's gullet and there, sitting in the whale's stomach, sitting at a table eating a fish dinner, is Geppetto.
Geppetto: Pinocchio, my dear son, I've found you at last. Where on earth have you been?
Narrator 3: Pinocchio tells his father all his adventures and together they plan their escape. They wait until the whale is a sleep and snoring and then they climb back up its gullet and out of its mouth.
Pinocchio: Hang on to me, Father. I'll save you. I'm made of wood so I can float.
Narrator 1: Eventually they reach land. By now poor Pinocchio is so weak he can hardly walk. Geppetto has to help him to get home.
Geppetto: Pinocchio, you rest now and in the morning you will feel a lot better.
Narrator 2: That night the Blue Fairy once again visited Geppetto's workshop.
Blue Fairy: Pinocchio, you have shown me that you have a good heart by being brave and putting your father before yourself. I shall forgive you forever being naughty. When you wake up you shall no longer made of wood but be a real live boy instead. I shall give you forty gold coins for your father, Geppetto.
Pinocchio: Father, Father, look at me. I'm not a naughty puppet anymore and I have all this money in my pocket.
Narrator 1: Geppetto could hardly believe his eyes and hugs his new son with joy.
Geppetto: Oh Pinocchio I'm so happy. Now we can begin our new life together. And we will never to be parted again,

The final play in this collection is based on Jules Verne's *Around the World in Eighty Days*

About the Author

Jules Verne (1828-1905)

Jules Verne was born on February 8, 1828, in Nantes, France. He is one of the found fathers of science fiction. Verne wrote his first novel *Five Weeks in a Balloon* in 1863 at the age of 35. During his lifetime he wrote over 70 novels. They included *Around the World in Eighty Days* (1873) and *Twenty Thousand Leagues under the Sea* (1870).Many of his stories involved technology that were fantasy for his time but they later became reality in the technological age. He died in 1905. In 2011, Google marked Jules Verne's 183rd birthday by featuring a Google doodle based on his works.

Around the World in Eighty Days

Characters: Four narrators, Phileas Fogg, Passepartout, Detective Fix, Princess, four club members, Bombay policeman, Calcutta policeman, elephant, elephant's guide, three acrobats, Judge, Brahmins, Captain, Captain 2.

Scene 1: The Reform Club
Narrator 1: In the year 1872, there lived a man called Phileas Fogg. He inhabited a house bearing the number seven in Saville Row, Burlington Gardens.
Narrator 2: All anyone knew about Phileas Fogg was that he was a member of the Reform Club.
Narrator 3: Fogg was a mysterious man. He spoke very little. He didn't seem to have any family. He lived with his French butler called Passepartout. No one ever visited number seven, Saville Row, Burlington Gardens.
Narrator 4: Every morning, he left his house at 11.30am and walked to the Reform Club. Every day he ate his lunch, read the newspaper and played cards. On the stroke of midnight, he would return home and go to bed. He did the same thing everyday.
(Phileas Fogg mimes walking to the club, eating his lunch, reading the paper, playing cards and returning home where he is greeted by Passepartout.)
Narrator 1: One day everything changed. He was at the club reading the newspaper when he stopped and said...
(He is sitting on a chair and there are three other club-members playing cards at a near-by table.)
Phileas Fogg: According to this article in the newspaper, it is possible to travel around the world in eighty day.
Club members: Ha, Ha.
Club member 1: Travel around the world in eighty days? That's impossible.

Club member 2: I never heard such rubbish.
Phileas Fogg: I think it may be possible.
Club member 3: I like to see you try.
Phileas Fogg: I would like nothing more than to travel around the world in eighty days.
Club member 1: Why don't we make a bet?
Club member 2: Here is £20,000. Take this money and see if you can travel around the world in eighty days.
Club member 3: If you are not back here in eighty days, you will need to pay us another £20,000.
Phileas Fogg: I accept the challenge and the wager. *(They all shake hands.)* The train to Dover leaves at 8.45pm. Today is the 2nd of October. I'll be back here on the 21st December at 8.45pm in the evening. *(He waves to them and returns home. Passepartout greets him and takes his hat.)*
Phileas Fogg: Passpartout, get packed; we are going around the world.
Passepartout: When?
Phileas Fogg: Now; just pack an overnight bag for both of us.
(They both go off stage.)
(Detective Fix enters the stage and he addresses the audience.)
Detective Fix: I am hunting a very dangerous thief. He stole £55,000 from the Bank of England. There is a large reward for his return—dead or alive He will try to leave England. I will go to the nearest port Dover and hunt him down.

Scene 2: **Dover Docks.**
(Passepartout comes on stage. Fix is skulking around investigating. Passepartout drops a passport. Detective Fix picks it up.)
Detective Fix: Is this your passport?
Passepartout: No, it is my master's. He stayed on board. He sent me here to get it stamped.

Detective Fix: *(Looks very carefully at the passport and then he addresses the audience.)* The man in the passport bears a strong resemblance to the thief. I have reason to believe the thief is on board. I will follow them very closely. *(Fix takes out his notebook and follows Phileas Fogg and Passepartout around the stage. The mime getting on and off the boat and looking at the different sights.)*
Detective Fix: Departed London, Wednesday, October 2nd, at 8.45 p.m. Arrived in Paris, Thursday, October 3rd, at 7.20 a.m. Left Paris, Thursday, at 8.40 a.m. Reached Turin by Mont Cenis, Friday, October 4th, at 6.35 a.m. Left Turin, Friday, at 7.20 a.m. Arrived at Brindisi, Saturday, October 5th, at 4 p.m. Embarked on the Mongolia, Saturday, at 5 p.m. Reached Suez, Wednesday, October 9th, at 11 a.m.
Narrator 2: One day, Fix saw Passepartout by himself.
Fix: Hello again. How are you enjoying your holiday? You seem to be in a great hurry.
Passpartout: I'm not in hurry it is my master who is in a rush?
Detective Fix: Where is your master going?
Passepartout: He says he is going around the world in eighty days.
Detective Fix: Around the world in eighty days but that is impossible.
Passepartout: Not according to my master.
Detective Fix: He must be very rich.
Passepartout: Well, he is carrying a large sum of money in new bank notes. He hasn't spared any money on the way. *(Passepartout leaves the stage.)*
Detective Fix: I must send a telegram to the chief of Scotland Yard in London. *(He reads out the telegram to the audience.)*I have no doubt I found our thief. He is pretending to be an eccentric who wants to travel around the world in eighty days. Send an arrest warrant to Bombay.

Narrator 3: The voyage was rough. Phileas Fogg didn't seem to mind. He ate four meals a day, read his newspaper and played cards. *(Fogg mimes doing all these activities.)*
Narrator 4: The ship was due to arrive in Bombay on the 22nd of October but arrived two days early on 20th.

Scene 3: India
Detective Fix: Where is the arrest warrant?
Bombay Policeman: You are early. The warrant hasn't arrived.
Detective Fix: My only hope is to stop Fogg from leaving India.
Phileas Fogg: Passepartout, we are catching the train to Calcutta tonight at 7pm. Take the rest of the day off and explore Bombay.
Narrator 1: Passepartout went sightseeing and came across a Pagoda.
Passepartout: What a beautiful a temple. I must go inside.
Narrator 2: He forgot to take off his shoes. He turned around a saw three angry priests.
Priest 1: How dare you not remove your shoes?
Priest 2: That's so disrespectful.
Priest 3: Quick, let's grab him and take off his shoes and socks.
Narrator 3: Passepartout fought off his attackers. He ran quickly without his shoes and socks and arrived at the train station just on time to catch the 7pm train to Calcutta. (*Detective Fix had followed Passepartout and had seen the fight.)*
Detective Fix: Now, I've seen the butler break the law I can arrested him along with his master.
Narrator 1: Phileas Fogg and Passepartout were sleeping on the train to Calcutta when suddenly it stopped and wouldn't move.
Fogg: Where are we?
Passepartout: Allahabad.
Phileas Fogg: How will we get to Calcutta?

Passepartout: I've an idea.
(He leaves the train and goes off stage. He comes back with an elephant and an elephant guide. They jump on the elephant and they continue on their journey.)
Narrator 3: After a while they came across a Brahmin procession.
Phileas Fogg: What is this?
Elephant Guide: A suttee?
Passepartout: What is a suttee?
Elephant Guide: It is a human sacrifice. The prince has died and tomorrow his wife will be burned to death beside her husband. It is the custom.
Phileas Fogg: We must save the princess. We have 12 hours to spare. We will stay the night. I have an idea. *(Fogg whispers in Passepartout's ear.)*
Narrator 4: The next morning, the dead prince was lying to the princess when suddenly he rose up like a ghost and grabbed the princess and ran.
Passepartout: Let's go.
Narrator 3: Passepartout had disguised himself as the dead prince in order to save the princess. *(The Brahmins chased them but they got away.)*
Narrator 1: Eventually they arrived in Calcutta.
Calcutta Policeman: You are under arrest.
Fogg and Passepartout: Why?
Calcutta Policeman: For fighting in the sacred temple.
(They arrive in court. The priests and the judge are there.)
Priests: *(Holding up shoes and socks.)* That is the man who disrespected our temple.
Passepartout: I'm so sorry about what happened at the temple. Please accept my apologies.
Phileas Fogg: Here is £2,000 for your trouble.
Priests: Thank you. Come to our temple anytime who wish.
Judge: Case dismissed.
Phileas Fogg: Quick Passepartout! We must run to get the boat to Hong Kong.

(They run off stage and Detective Fix comes on stage. He looks very angry.)
Detective Fix: Drat! Foiled again. I know, I will follow them to Hong Kong. Hong Kong is British and I can arrest them there.

Scene 4: Hong Kong
Narrator 1: They arrived in Hong Kong.
Phileas Fogg: Passepartout, we are going to find somewhere to stay tonight. You stay here and book three cabins on the ship to Yokohama, Japan, for tomorrow morning.
Narrator 2: When Passepartout went to book the cabins, he found out that the ship was leaving that night.
Detective Fix: Hello again. You seem in a hurry.
Passepartout: The ship is leaving tonight. I must tell my master.
Detective Fix: You have plenty of time. Come with me to the inn and we can have a drink.
(They go to the inn and drink.)
Detective Fix: I'm a detective and your master is a thief.
Passepartout: Nonsense.
Detective Fix: You must not tell him that the ship leaves tonight. Have another drink.
Narrator 3: After a few drinks Passepartout was drunk and fell asleep. Detective Fix left him there.
Next morning, the princess and Phileas Fogg arrived at the port. There was no sign of the ship or Passepartout.
Phileas Fogg: Where is the ship?
Princess: Where is Passepartout?
Phileas Fogg: He must have gone on ahead of us.
Captain: The ship to Yokohama left last night.
(Detective Fix arrives on the dock.)
Detective Fix: I missed the ship too and there isn't another steamer leaving until next week.

Captain: I have a boat. I'm going to Shanghai but I can go quickly and catch up with the steamer. It will cost you £500.
Fogg: It is a deal. *(They shake hands and turns to Fix.)*Would you like to join us?
Fix: Oh yes, please.
Narrator 4: They sailed for two days. The seas were very rough and Detective Fix was violently sick. *(He gets sick over the side of the boat.)*
Captain: Look over there, there is the steamer. Stop! Everybody out.
Narrator 1: Fogg, the princess and Fix clamoured on board of the steamer. Meanwhile back on the Hong Kong boat quay...
Passepartout: Where's Fogg and the princess? They must have gone ahead without me.
(Enter three acrobats. They do cartwheels and some gymnastic moves.)
Acrobat1: What's wrong? You look sad.
Passepartout: My master and the princess have left me here by myself.
Acrobat 2: Where are they going?
Passepartout: Japan but then on to America.
Acrobat 3: We are going to America. Come with us.
Acrobat 1: Can you stand on your head?
Passepartout: Yes!
Acrobat 2: Can you stand on one leg?
Passepartout: Yes!
Acrobat 3: You're in. Welcome to the troupe. *(They all hug.)*

Scene 5: America
Narrator 2: The acrobats and Passepartout reached America. One night while they were performing Phileas Fogg and the princess were in the audience.
Fogg: Oh my goodness, is that Passepartout?
Princess: Yes, it is.

Fogg and Princess: Passepartout over here. *(They wave.)*
Passepartout: At last, I found you. I missed you.
Fogg and Princess: We missed you too. *(They hug.)*
Narrator 1: They travelled around the Americas by boat, train and sled. All the while Detective Fix followed closely behind.*(This is performed in a mime sequence.)*
Narrator 2: Eventually they arrived in New York. The ship to England had left a day early.
Narrator 3: Once again Fogg found a captain of a ship.
Captain 2: I will take you to France for a price.
Fogg: It is a deal. *(Shakes hands.)*
Narrator 4: When they were on board the ship, Fogg locked the captain up, and changed the course of the ship towards Liverpool.
Fogg: Look Passepartout. It's Liverpool we are on time.
Passepartout: You will win the bet now.

Scene 6: England
Narrator 1: They stepped off the boat in just enough time to get to London. However, Detective Fix arrived with some policeman.
Detective Fix: Phileas Fogg, you are under arrest.
Fogg: What for?
Detective Fix: For stealing £55,000.
Narrator 2: The police threw him into jail.
Princess: Passepartout what will we do?
Passepartout: I don't think there is anything we can do. He will lose the bet.
Narrator 3: After a few hours, Detective Fix returned to the prison cell.
Detective Fix: I've made a dreadful mistake. The real thief was arrested three days ago. You are free to go.
Fogg: Quick, Princess and Passepartout, if we rush we can catch the train to London.
(They run and jump on the train and arrived in London.)
Passepartout: Fogg, look at the clock. It is 8.55pm. You have lost the bet by 10 mins.

Narrator 4: The next day, Fogg spent the day adding up how much he had spent. Suddenly he looked at the calendar. It is the 21st of December today. How did that happen?

Passepartout: We gained a day by travelling from East to West.

Fogg: So, I haven't lost the bet. *(Looks at the clock.)* Quick, we have 10 minutes to reach the Reform Club.*(Phileas Fogg, Passepartout and the princess all race to the Reform Club where they are greeted and congratulated by the four club members.)*

All Narrators: Fogg won the £ 20,000 but since he spent £19, 000 on the way, he wasn't much better off.

73140328R00050

Made in the USA
Columbia, SC
05 July 2017